INSIDE THE NBA

CHARLOTTE HORNETS

BY DAVID J. CLARKE

SportsZone
An Imprint of Abdo Publishing
abdobooks.com

abdobooks.com

Published by Abdo Publishing, a division of ABDO, PO Box 398166, Minneapolis, Minnesota 55439. Copyright © 2023 by Abdo Consulting Group, Inc. International copyrights reserved in all countries. No part of this book may be reproduced in any form without written permission from the publisher. SportsZone™ is a trademark and logo of Abdo Publishing.

Printed in China.
052022
092022

Cover Photo: Jacob Kupferman/AP Images
Interior Photos: Melinda Nagy/Shutterstock Images, 1; Jacob Kupferman/Getty Images Sport/Getty Images, 4; Louis Lopez/Modern Exposure/Cal Sport Media/ZUMA Wire/AP Images, 7; Jacob Kupferman/AP Images, 9; Jared C. Tilton/Getty Images Sport/Getty Images, 11; Focus on Sport/Getty Images Sport/Getty Images, 12, 16, 27, 34; Jim Gund/Getty Images Sport/Getty Images, 15; Chuck Burton/AP Images, 19, 21; Hakim Wright Sr./AP Images, 22; Winslow Townson/AP Images, 24; Rick Havner/AP Images, 29; Jeffrey Phelps/AP Images, 30; Anthony Au-Yeung/Getty Images Sport/Getty Images, 33; Al Messerschmidt/AP Images, 36; John Raoux/AP Images, 38; Wilfredo Lee/AP Images, 39; Derick Hingle/AP Images, 41

Editor: Charlie Beattie
Series Designer: Joshua Olson

Library of Congress Control Number: 2021951671

Publisher's Cataloging-in-Publication Data

Names: Clarke, David J., author.
Title: Charlotte Hornets / by David J. Clarke
Description: Minneapolis, Minnesota : Abdo Publishing, 2023 | Series: Inside the NBA | Includes online resources and index.
Identifiers: ISBN 9781532198212 (lib. bdg.) | ISBN 9781098271862 (ebook)
Subjects: LCSH: Charlotte Hornets (Basketball team : 2014-)--Juvenile literature. | Basketball--Juvenile literature. | Professional sports--Juvenile literature. | Sports franchises--Juvenile literature.
Classification: DDC 796.32364--dc23

TABLE OF CONTENTS

CHAPTER ONE
A WHOLE NEW BALL GAME..... 4

CHAPTER TWO
HORNETS HISTORY 12

CHAPTER THREE
CHARLOTTE'S SHOOTING STARS 24

CHAPTER FOUR
HORNETS HIGHLIGHTS 34

TIMELINE 42
TEAM FACTS 44
TEAM TRIVIA 45
GLOSSARY 46
MORE INFORMATION 47
ONLINE RESOURCES 47
INDEX 48
ABOUT THE AUTHOR 48

CHAPTER ONE

A WHOLE NEW BALL GAME

Charlotte Hornets fans held their breath. Adam Silver walked to the podium holding a large envelope. In mere moments, the National Basketball Association (NBA) commissioner would read a name that could change the course of the long-suffering franchise. But would it be the name many of them expected?

The NBA Draft is one of the most important events in the off-season. It's when all the teams get to select new players who are entering the league. Teams who struggled the previous season are higher in the draft order. If a team makes the right selection, its fortunes can change overnight.

The Hornets were one of those struggling teams after the 2019–20 season. They had not made the playoffs in five years. The fans in Charlotte had not seen a playoff series victory in nearly two decades. Attendance was low at games, despite basketball being wildly popular in North Carolina.

LaMelo Ball's arrival before the 2020–21 season created newfound excitement in Charlotte.

Charlotte supporters hoped the draft would give them something to look forward to.

The 2020 draft didn't have an obvious first choice. Many experts said one of any three players were worthy of the pick. Many Hornets fans had just one player in mind, though. They watched as Silver came out to announce the first pick. The Minnesota Timberwolves selected guard Anthony Edwards. Next, the Golden State Warriors grabbed center James Wiseman. That left the one player many Hornets fans wanted still on the board. Finally, Silver opened the envelope to reveal whether their wish had come true.

"With the third pick in the 2020 NBA Draft," Silver read, "the Charlotte Hornets select LaMelo Ball from Chino Hills, California."

THE PHENOM ARRIVES

Although he was young, Ball was already famous in basketball circles. He had been talked about as a future star since he

A Rebellious Name

The image of a hornet's nest has long been a symbol for the city of Charlotte. And that made the nickname "Hornets" an easy choice for the franchise in 1988. One story says the name dates to the American Revolution (1775–1783). The Battle of Charlotte was fought in 1780. After the battle, British general George Cornwallis supposedly referred to the Charlotte area as "a hornet's nest of rebellion." No one knows if this story is true, but it has stuck through the years.

Long before he was a professional, Ball was a highly rated high school player in Chino Hills, California.

was 12 years old. His older brother Lonzo was already an NBA standout. The brothers' outspoken father, LaVar, had long been hyping up his sons on social media or to anyone who asked.

Hornets fans were thrilled to have a player who might be special. The 6-foot-7-inch guard was a dangerous scoring threat. But he also had great passing ability. Some scouts compared him to former NBA great point guards Jason Kidd and Anfernee Hardaway.

The NBA season started a month later. And Ball took some time to get going. In the first three games, he scored only 19 points. As a point guard, he was asked to handle the ball and pass it to teammates. But he had nearly as many turnovers as assists.

BALL TAKES OVER

After a few games, though, Ball began showing signs of the player many hoped he could be. Ball was a unique playmaker. He could shoot and pass. Yet he also used his size to grab a lot of rebounds. He looked like a threat to achieve a triple-double on any night.

In fact, on January 8, 2021, he almost did just that. Ball fell just short with 12 points, 10 rebounds, and nine assists in a 118–110 win over the New Orleans Pelicans. He did it playing against his older brother Lonzo, the Pelicans point guard.

The Hornets were back in action the next night, this time against the Atlanta Hawks. Ball was still coming off the bench. Charlotte coach James Borrego didn't want to rush Ball's development. But whenever the rookie came in, he seemed to make a difference. The Hornets were trailing 16–13 halfway through the first quarter when Ball finally entered against Atlanta. He went to work immediately.

One minute later Ball took a pass from teammate Gordon Hayward. After a quick jab step toward the basket,

Ball's size and passing ability created a rare combination for an NBA player and drew comparisons to past NBA greats.

Ball pulled back. He had spotted something. Teammate Terry Rozier III was cutting along the baseline. Ball flung a one-handed pass to Rozier for a layup.

On the next possession, Ball was dribbling outside the three-point line. Suddenly a gap opened in the defense. The rookie exploded down the lane for an easy layup of his own. It was his only basket of the first quarter. But Ball was showing his full range of skills. He dished out another assist and grabbed three rebounds.

Ball truly took over the game late in the second quarter. The Hawks led 44–43 with 4:18 to go when Ball backed down his defender from the top of the key. At the free-throw line, he suddenly stopped, spun, and put up a fadeaway jumper. It hit nothing but net.

Ball was just getting warmed up. He either scored or assisted on all six baskets the Hornets had the rest of the quarter. Charlotte built a nine-point lead going into the locker room. The phenom had nine points, seven assists, and four rebounds. Those watching the game started to wonder if a triple-double was possible.

HISTORY IN THE MAKING

The second half was more of the same. When defenders got too close, Ball drove past them for easy baskets. If they sagged off, he hit long jump shots. He drove the lane and dished to open teammates for layups and dunks. It was clear the Hornets were a better team when he was playing. The rookie was controlling the game.

With 6:13 left in the fourth quarter, Ball took control at the top of the key. Charlotte forward P. J. Washington came out to set a screen. As Ball went around it, Washington wheeled away toward the basket. Both defenders moved to Ball, so he threw a quick pass over them. Washington snagged it and knocked down a short jumper. It was a perfectly executed pick-and-roll.

It also made history. Ball already had 21 points. A few minutes earlier he pulled in his tenth rebound. His pass to Washington gave Ball 10 assists. He was 19 years, 140 days old. At the time, that made Ball the youngest player to ever record an NBA triple-double.

Ball's final totals were 22 points, 12 rebounds, and 11 assists. He turned the ball over only once. The Hornets won the game 113–105.

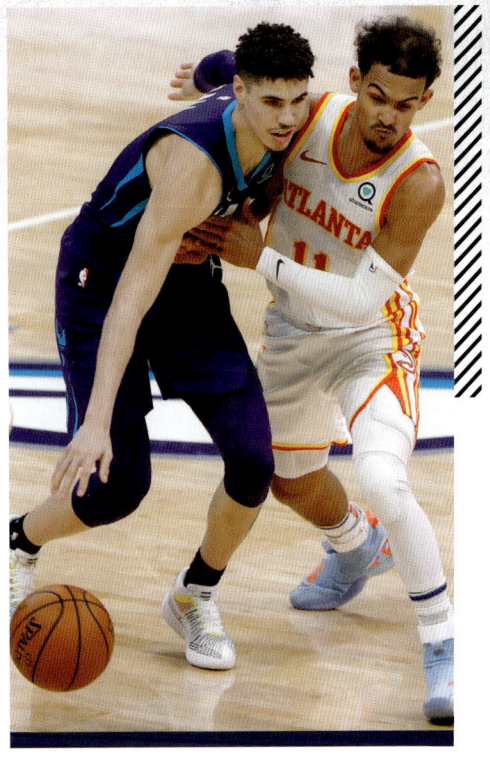

Ball, *left*, dribbles against Atlanta guard Trae Young during the Charlotte rookie's record-setting performance in January 2021.

Perhaps most importantly, Ball's effort propelled Charlotte to its third win in a row. The Hornets finished the year 33–39. That was 10 wins better than the year before. Charlotte might have finished even stronger if Ball had not broken his wrist in March. The injury caused him to miss 21 games. He still played well enough to win the NBA Rookie of the Year Award at the end of the season.

Ball was more than worth the wait for Charlotte fans. They now had a star on the floor. They also had hope in the stands.

11

CHAPTER TWO

HORNETS HISTORY

North Carolina has long been a basketball hotbed. Division I college programs are everywhere in the state. That includes powerhouses such as Duke University and the University of North Carolina. NBA legends including Walt Bellamy, James Worthy, and Michael Jordan all grew up in the state. For many years, the one thing that was missing was a successful pro team.

During the 1960s and 1970s, a new league called the American Basketball Association (ABA) tried to compete with the NBA. Among the ABA teams were the Carolina Cougars, who split their time among three North Carolina cities, including Charlotte. But the Cougars moved in 1974, and the ABA folded two years later. The city was again without pro basketball. In 1985 local entrepreneur George Shinn wanted to change that. Shinn was from Kannapolis, which is

Sharpshooting Dell Curry was an original Hornet and spent a decade with the team.

The Hive

The Hornets' first home court was the Charlotte Coliseum. In fact, the huge arena was a major reason the NBA decided to give the city a team in the first place. Known as "the Hive," the Coliseum was the largest stadium in the league. It held 24,000 fans. And Hornets fans came out in big numbers. They were either first or second in NBA attendance every year from 1988–89 to 1997–98.

near Charlotte. Expansion teams have to pay large sums of money to the league before they are allowed to join. Shinn and his business partners were wealthy enough to pay $32.5 million to get Charlotte into the league.

The Hornets were ready to start playing in 1988. But they needed players. On June 23, 1988, the NBA held an expansion draft for Charlotte and the league's other new team, the Miami Heat. Existing NBA teams are allowed to protect their best players from the expansion draft. Most players picked are not likely to make a lasting impact on the team. However, two players the Hornets drafted stuck with the team for years. Shooting guard Dell Curry and point guard Muggsy Bogues each spent 10 seasons in Charlotte.

The original Hornets roster was filled with experienced players. Forward Kelly Tripucka had been a high-scoring player in his career. Power forward Kurt Rambis had been an NBA champion with the Los Angeles Lakers. Led by coach Dick Harter, the team hoped the veteran core would lead to early

Despite having experienced players like Kurt Rambis on the roster, the Hornets struggled during their early seasons.

success. But the plan didn't pan out. The Hornets finished their first season with a 20–62 record.

L. J. AND ZO

Despite playing in front of record crowds, the Hornets had losing records for their first four seasons. But they picked up their first young stars through the NBA Draft in 1991 and 1992. Larry Johnson was short for a power forward at 6 feet, 7 inches. But he was built like a tank. He also had quick moves and handled the ball well for a big man. He was an instant star after the Hornets took him with the top pick in 1991.

A year later the Hornets picked second overall, and this time they got a star center. Alonzo Mourning was a powerful

Alonzo Mourning (33) and fellow rising star Larry Johnson (2) helped turn Charlotte into one of the NBA's most exciting teams in the early 1990s.

player in the low post on offense and defense. He needed only 49 games of his rookie season to set the Hornets record for career blocks.

With the two young stars on board and a veteran backcourt of Bogues and Curry, the Hornets were ready to improve. The team won 44 games in 1992–93 and reached the playoffs for the first time. But it was a close call. With five games left, the Hornets were in seventh place. They needed a strong finish to make sure they made the playoffs. Charlotte won all five games and qualified fifth in the Eastern Conference.

Charlotte made its playoff stay memorable. The Hornets lost their first game to the favored Boston Celtics. But Charlotte rebounded to take Game 2 in double overtime. It was the first playoff win in team history. Two games later they won their first series. Mourning finished Game 4 with 33 points. And his 20-foot shot with 0.4 seconds left won the game 104–103.

Charlotte lost in the second round to the New York Knicks. But the young team appeared to be on the rise. Though they missed the playoffs in 1993–94, the Hornets were back the next season. Their 50 wins in the regular season set a team record. But the Hornets had to take on the powerful Chicago Bulls. The Bulls were led by the high-scoring Jordan, the best player of his era. They had won three straight NBA titles from 1991 to 1993. Jordan then retired to try professional baseball. After 18 months away from basketball, he had just returned. Picking up where he left off, Jordan led the Bulls to a four-game series victory.

By this time, the Hornets' two young stars were having trouble getting along. Johnson had just received the biggest contract in NBA history. Mourning thought his contract should be higher than Johnson's. But Shinn said he did not have enough to pay both players. So in the off-season, the Hornets traded Mourning to the Miami Heat for shooting guard Glen Rice and three other players. But it was not enough to keep the Hornets in the playoffs. They missed out after finishing 41–41.

STARTING OVER AGAIN

Head coach Allan Bristow was fired. But even more surprisingly, Johnson was traded too. He went to the Knicks. Yet even with their young stars gone, Charlotte improved. Rice and Curry were two of the league's best shooters. Center Vlade Divac joined the team from the Lakers. Power forward Anthony Mason came over from the Knicks to provide hustle.

The 1996–97 Hornets surprised the league and won 54 games. The problem was that the NBA's Eastern Conference had several great teams. That record only secured Charlotte the number six seed. It had to face the mighty Knicks in the first round. And New York swept the Hornets right out of the playoffs.

The Hornets remained competitive for the rest of the 1990s but never won more than a series in the playoffs. By 2000 their fan support was starting to fade. The Charlotte Coliseum was not selling out anymore. Shinn wanted the city to help pay for a new, fancier arena. But the local government would not do it.

Shinn threatened to move the team if he did not get his way. Charlotte officials refused to budge. Fans, angry at

Guard David Wesley walks off the floor after the Hornets' final home game before moving to New Orleans. It was an 89–79 playoff loss to the New Jersey Nets on May 12, 2002.

Shinn, stopped showing up at the Hive, as Charlotte's arena was nicknamed. After the 2001–02 season, Shinn moved the Hornets to New Orleans. A decade earlier the Hornets had been the best game in town. Now they were gone.

Fans were devastated. But they did not have to wait long for basketball to return. Just two years later the NBA awarded a new expansion team to Charlotte. Television executive Robert

Johnson bid $300 million to bring basketball back. But the team could not be called the Hornets. That name belonged to New Orleans. The new team would be named the Bobcats and donned navy blue and orange uniforms.

Charlotte started over with a new expansion draft. The Bobcats' first season did not go well. They won only 18 games. Despite having talented young players like guard Gerald Wallace and center Emeka Okafor, Charlotte struggled for years. The team didn't make the playoffs until the 2009–10 season. That year the Bobcats were swept in the first round by the Orlando Magic.

Groundbreaker

Robert Johnson wasn't just another billionaire when he bought the Charlotte Bobcats. Johnson was the first Black majority owner in American professional sports in nearly 50 years. Johnson was also the first Black owner to own a professional team outside of baseball's defunct Negro Leagues. When Johnson sold the Bobcats in 2010, Michael Jordan became the second Black majority owner in the NBA.

BACK TO THE HIVE

During that season, another owner was ready to take over. NBA legend Michael Jordan had bought a small stake in the team a few years earlier. Now he was ready to buy Johnson's share. On February 27, 2010, Jordan became the first former NBA player to own a team.

Jordan brought attention to the team, but the Bobcats still

Michael Jordan, *left*, announces the team's decision to change its name back to the Hornets in May 2013.

struggled. They missed the playoffs for three consecutive years. The 2011–12 team was one of the worst the NBA had ever seen. That year Charlotte finished 7–59.

Two years later the Bobcats were back in the playoffs. And they had a young star in guard Kemba Walker. But they were swept in the first round again. This time it was by the Heat. A Charlotte basketball team had not won a playoff game in 12 years.

However, the team was once again making headlines off the court. In 2013 the New Orleans team changed its name to the Pelicans. When they did, Jordan asked the league if Charlotte could have the Hornets nickname back. After the 2013–14

High-flying forward Miles Bridges throws down a dunk during a 2021 game against the Atlanta Hawks.

season ended, a deal was made with New Orleans. Charlotte bought back the name and the team's original history.

The Hornets also went back to their original uniform colors. The team adopted the slogan "Buzz City" to generate excitement. But Walker was providing most of the thrills. Many thought the 6-foot guard was too small to be an NBA superstar. But he averaged more than 20 points per game during the 2015–16 season. In January of that year, he set a team record by scoring 52 points in one game.

The team finished 48–34 and reached the playoffs. It was the best record Charlotte had seen since 1999–2000. The season ended in a familiar way, though. The Hornets pushed the favored Heat to a seventh game but couldn't close out the series. With that loss, Charlotte's drought without a playoff series win reached 14 seasons. And even though the team was promising, they could not stay in the playoff picture. Charlotte missed the postseason each of the next five years.

In 2019 Walker was traded to the Boston Celtics. The Hornets were starting over once again. The team picked up young talent like forward Miles Bridges and guards Terry Rozier III and LaMelo Ball. Charlotte fans were building the buzz again. They hoped that this time the young stars could deliver playoff success.

CHAPTER THREE

CHARLOTTE'S SHOOTING STARS

Charlotte picked up several veterans in the 1988 expansion draft. Many did not stick around long. But Dell Curry ended up playing a decade for the Hornets. Curry was a smooth three-point shooter who was the team's all-time leading scorer until his record was broken in 2018. However, these days he's perhaps best known for passing on his shooting skills to his two sons, Seth and Steph. Seth became an NBA regular. Steph became one of the league's all-time best three-point shooters and won back-to-back NBA Most Valuable Player (MVP) Awards in 2015 and 2016.

The other half of Charlotte's original backcourt was Tyrone "Muggsy" Bogues. The point guard had North Carolina ties even before he was a Hornet. He played college basketball a short drive away from Charlotte at Wake Forest University.

Larry Johnson, *left*, and Muggsy Bogues were two of the Hornets' earliest stars.

Bogues stood out on the basketball court. At 5 feet, 3 inches tall, he was the shortest man ever to wear an NBA uniform. But Bogues's lack of height never held him back. In fact, he often used his short stature to his advantage. He was never a top scorer, but Bogues enjoyed a long NBA career because of his quickness, passing ability, and tough defense. His improbable success made him one of the most beloved players in NBA history.

YOUNG GUNS

All of that losing in the Hornets' early years did have some benefits. In 1991 the team earned the first pick in the draft. With it, Charlotte selected forward Larry Johnson. The quick, strong power forward brought both skills and swagger to Charlotte. In 1993 "L. J." became the first Hornets player selected for the NBA All-Star Game.

One year later the Hornets had the second draft pick. With it they selected center Alonzo Mourning. A college star at Georgetown University, Mourning was a dominant force from day one in the NBA. He averaged more than 20 points, 10 rebounds, and three blocked shots per game his rookie year. However, he missed out on the Rookie of the Year Award to the Orlando Magic's Shaquille O'Neal.

Mourning and Johnson's relationship soured after a few years together. Both were eventually traded. But for three

Alonzo Mourning boxes out during a game against the New York Knicks.

seasons they helped Charlotte compete with the NBA's best. Johnson's flashy dunks and Mourning's inside power scared the rest of the NBA. However, Hornets fans never got the chance to see what they could become together.

Bobby Phills

The Hornets signed guard Bobby Phills in the summer of 1997. He was a gritty defender and an accurate shooter who helped the team make the playoffs in his first season. He was also well respected in the Charlotte community for his charity work. Phills was in his third season with the team in January 2000 when he died in a car crash. His No. 13 jersey is the only retired number in Charlotte Hornets history.

Most teams suffer in the standings when players like Johnson and Mourning are traded. Charlotte actually improved without the two stars. The 1996–97 Hornets put up the team's best-ever record at 54–28. It was a true group effort.

Getting Glen Rice for Mourning helped. The 6-foot-7-inch forward had one of the best shooting strokes in the NBA. That year he averaged a career-high 26.8 points per game. With Rice and Curry leading the way, the Hornets were the best three-point shooting team in the league. Rice was also the league's best individual three-point shooter.

The player who came from the Knicks for Johnson provided the muscle inside. Power forward Anthony Mason was one of the NBA's toughest players. That season he never seemed to come off the court. Mason led the NBA, averaging over 43 minutes per game. The other key piece of Charlotte's front line was center Vlade Divac. The 7-foot-1-inch Serbian could score. He was also skilled at passing the ball to open outside shooters.

Charlotte's Gerald Wallace (3) rises for a dunk against the Detroit Pistons in 2008.

Kemba Walker fights his way to the hoop against the Milwaukee Bucks during a 2019 game.

Leading the team was a new head coach. Dave Cowens was a Hall of Fame center for the Boston Celtics in the 1970s. He had even coached the Celtics while still a player during the 1978–79 season. But that was his only year serving as a head coach, until the Hornets hired him in 1996. That inexperience didn't matter. Cowens coached Charlotte for only two full seasons. But he won 60 percent of his games and made the playoffs both years.

SEARCHING FOR A STAR

The Hornets left Charlotte after the 2001–02 season. When the Bobcats were formed in 2004, they had to do the expansion draft all over again. Gerald Wallace was the only player Charlotte selected who made a lasting impact. Wallace had been a bench player for the Sacramento Kings. But he blossomed as a scorer after arriving in Charlotte. The guard spent seven seasons with the Bobcats. He helped them reach the playoffs for the first time in 2009–10. In the 10 seasons Charlotte spent as the Bobcats, Wallace was the only player on the team to play in the All-Star Game.

The Hornets/Bobcats struggled to draft impact players throughout most of their history. But they did have some luck picking players from the University of Connecticut (UConn). Emeka Okafor was the Bobcats' first-ever draft pick in 2004. The reliable center was named the NBA's Rookie of the Year in 2005. Ankle injuries began to slow him down the next season. But Okafor proved to be effective and consistent. He averaged

What Might Have Been

The greatest player Charlotte ever drafted never played a minute for the Hornets. In 1996 the team selected high schooler Kobe Bryant with the thirteenth pick. The young guard had already told Charlotte he would not play for them. But Charlotte took Bryant so it could trade him for center Vlade Divac of the Los Angeles Lakers. Divac spent two seasons as a productive and popular player in Charlotte. But Bryant developed into one of the NBA's greatest ever.

a double-double in each of his five years in Charlotte. When he left the team in 2009, Okafor was the franchise's all-time leading rebounder.

Another former UConn Husky who made it big in Charlotte was Kemba Walker. The guard had just led UConn to the national championship when Charlotte picked him ninth in the 2011 draft. Despite standing only 6 feet tall, Walker developed into a lethal scorer. He carried the Hornets back into the playoffs in 2014 and 2016. On their second trip, Walker's scoring nearly knocked out the heavily favored Miami Heat. But like the Hornets' other stars, Walker eventually left the team. When he did so in 2019, he was the only player to have earned more than 10,000 career points with Charlotte.

Unlike Okafor and Walker, the Hornets' next star never played in college. Instead LaMelo Ball played against professionals in foreign leagues. When he was 16 years old, he left to play professionally in the European country of Lithuania. He returned to the United States for his senior year, but then

LaMelo Ball took a unique route to the NBA, including a year playing professionally in Australia.

he decided to pass on college basketball. The year before he was drafted, he played for the Illawarra Hawks of Australia's National Basketball League. That experience helped the teenage point guard win Rookie of the Year in 2020–21. With Ball running the team's offense, the future was looking up in Buzz City.

CHAPTER FOUR

HORNETS HIGHLIGHTS

The Hornets played to sold-out crowds every night when they joined the NBA. With 24,000 fans in the stands, the Hive was one of the NBA's loudest arenas.

That was especially true on December 23, 1988. That night the Hornets were facing Michael Jordan and the Chicago Bulls for the first time. Jordan had grown up across the state in Wilmington, North Carolina. By 1988 he was the most dominant player in the NBA. The basketball great didn't disappoint. Jordan led all scorers with 33 points. But Charlotte forward Kelly Tripucka nearly matched him with 30 of his own.

The game came down to the final seconds. Charlotte forward Kurt Rambis sent the crowd into a frenzy when his put-back layup at the buzzer won the game 103–101 for the Hornets.

Forward Kelly Tripucka led the Hornets in scoring during their first season, averaging 22.6 points per game.

In the 1993 playoffs, Alonzo Mourning, *left*, made a closing shot that thrilled Charlotte fans.

POSTSEASON BUZZ

Wins like the one against the Bulls were hard to come by in the first few years. But with the additions of Larry Johnson and Alonzo Mourning, Charlotte was a playoff team by the 1992–93 season.

Mourning provided the first lasting playoff memory for Charlotte fans. The Hornets led the Boston Celtics 2–1 in the best-of-five first round series. But Charlotte trailed 103–102 with three seconds left in Game 4. Charlotte was inbounding underneath its offensive basket. Suddenly, Mourning was open at the top of the key. Dell Curry fired him a pass. Mourning stepped back once and hit a long jumper to win the game and the series.

Grandmama

Larry Johnson was a star on the court in the early 1990s. But his "Grandmama" was an even bigger star off it. The character was invented by the Converse shoe company for Johnson's commercials. Grandmama was Johnson dressed up as an elderly woman. She told funny basketball-themed nursery rhymes over video of Grandmama dunking basketballs. The line of commercials was one of the most popular in NBA history.

Knocked onto his back after the shot, Mourning stayed down on the floor with his arms in the air. Teammates, coaches, and even the Hornets mascot, Hugo, piled on him in celebration.

GOODBYE, HELLO

It took only two years after the Hornets left Charlotte for basketball to return. When the Bobcats started playing in 2004, one of their most anticipated games was the return of the New Orleans Hornets.

Emeka Okafor had 20 points and 12 rebounds in Charlotte's victory over the New Orleans Hornets on December 14, 2004.

The teams met in Charlotte on December 14, 2004. Both were struggling entering the game. The Bobcats were just 5–14. New Orleans was even worse at 1–19. Still, more than 13,000 fans showed up. The team offered any fan who wanted one a free Bobcats hat if they traded in old Charlotte Hornets gear.

The game was close throughout and went to overtime. With seven seconds left, New Orleans led 93–92. Bobcats rookie center Emeka Okafor drove the lane and drew a foul. Shaking off the pressure, he sank both free throws for the lead. New Orleans had one chance left, but guard Junior Harrington's jumper missed the mark as the horn sounded.

"You could sense the fans wanted it," Okafor said after the game. "They wanted us to beat the Hornets, and we sensed it meant a lot to the city."

Guards Courtney Lee, *left*, and Jeremy Lin celebrate after Lee's dramatic three-point shot against the Miami Heat in the 2016 playoffs.

BUZZ CITY

Playoff appearances were few and far between during the Bobcats years. Charlotte reached the postseason only twice with that nickname. And they never made it out of the first round.

After taking the Hornets nickname back, the team reached the playoffs again after the 2015–16 season. They faced the favored Miami Heat in the first round. Charlotte took a 3–2 lead in dramatic style.

Miami led 88–87 with less than 40 seconds remaining, but Hornets star Kemba Walker had a good chance at a jumper. The shot missed, but guard Courtney Lee swooped in from the corner to grab the offensive rebound. Lee dribbled past the three-point line and threw a quick pass to Jeremy Lin. Realizing Lee was wide open, Lin tossed it right back. Lee drained a three-pointer to give Charlotte a 90–88 lead.

Lee was not a likely hero. He had just joined the team in a February trade from the Memphis Grizzlies. In 28 games in Charlotte, he had averaged 8.9 points. But he was not done with his playoff heroics. Miami had one more chance, and the ball fell to star guard Dwyane Wade near the basket with three seconds left. He looked like he had a layup. Lee swooped in and rejected the shot to seal the victory.

BROTHER BATTLE

The Hornets could not close out Miami. The Heat won the last two games of the series. Charlotte drifted out of the playoff picture for the next few seasons, but hope arrived when LaMelo Ball joined the team in 2020.

LaMelo Ball, *left*, **plays defense against his older brother Lonzo in the brothers' first meeting as NBA players.**

Basketball fans watched with interest when the Hornets faced the New Orleans Pelicans on January 8, 2021. But this time, Hornets fans weren't worried about beating the city that took their team so long ago. This meeting was the first matchup between LaMelo and his older brother Lonzo.

The Hornets rallied from 18 points down in the first half to win 118–110. And LaMelo easily won the battle of the brothers. Lonzo finished with only five points. The younger Ball put up 12, along with 10 rebounds and nine assists. Though his historic triple-double had to wait one more day, LaMelo was creating a buzz in Buzz City.

TIMELINE

1987
The NBA grants a franchise to Charlotte. The team chooses the Hornets as its nickname.

1988
The Hornets play their first game on November 4. They lose 133–93 to the Cleveland Cavaliers. Their first win comes four days later against the Los Angeles Clippers.

1991
The Hornets use the number one draft pick on forward Larry Johnson.

1992
Charlotte selects Alonzo Mourning second overall in the draft. The center teams up with Johnson to form one of the NBA's most potent player combinations.

1993
Mourning's dramatic late shot in Game 4 of the Hornets' opening-round playoff series clinches a victory over the Boston Celtics.

1997
With Johnson and Mourning gone from the team, guard Glen Rice leads the Hornets to 54 wins, the most in team history.